→INTRODUCING

ARTIFICIAL INTELLIGENCE

HENRY BRIGHTON & HOWARD SELINA

This edition published in
the UK and the USA
in 2010 by Icon Books Ltd,
Omnibus Business Centre,
39–41 North Road, London N7 9DP
email: info@iconbooks.com
www.introducingbooks.com

Sold in the UK, Europe and Asia
by Faber & Faber Ltd,
Bloomsbury House,
74–77 Great Russell Street,
London WC1B 3DA or their agents

Distributed in South Africa
by Jonathan Ball,
Office B4, The District,
41 Sir Lowry Road,
Woodstock 7925

Distributed in Australia and
New Zealand
by Allen & Unwin Pty Ltd,
PO Box 8500,
83 Alexander Street,
Crows Nest, NSW 2065

Distributed in the USA
by Publishers Group West,
1700 Fourth Street,
Berkeley, CA 94710

Distributed in Canada
by Publishers Group Canada,
76 Stafford Street, Unit 300
Toronto, Ontario M6J 2S1

Previously published in the UK and
Australia in 2003 under the current title

ISBN: 978-184831-214-2

Originating editor: Richard Appignanesi

Printed by Clays Ltd, St Ives plc

Artificial Intelligence

Over the past half-century there has been intense research into the construction of intelligent machinery – the problem of creating *Artificial Intelligence*. This research has resulted in chess-playing computers capable of beating the best players, and humanoid robots able to negotiate novel environments and interact with people.

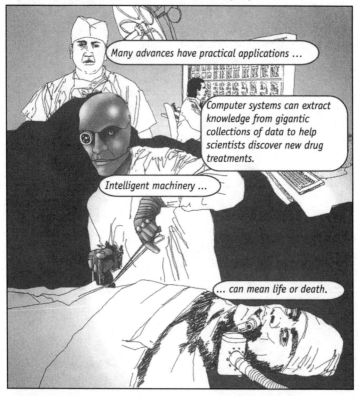

Computer systems are installed at airports to sniff luggage for explosives. Military hardware is becoming increasingly reliant on research into intelligent machinery: missiles now find their targets with the aid of machine vision systems.

Defining the AI Problem

Research into Artificial Intelligence, or AI, has resulted in successful engineering projects. But perhaps more importantly, AI raises questions that extend way beyond engineering applications.

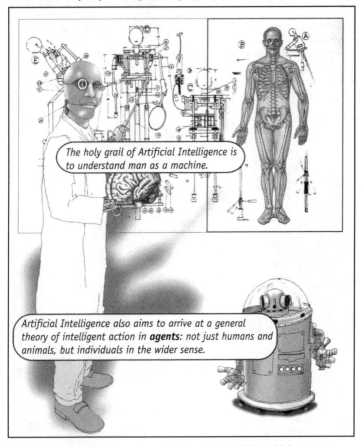

The capabilities of an agent could extend beyond that which we can currently imagine. This is an exceptionally bold enterprise which tackles, head-on, philosophical arguments which have been raging for thousands of years.

What Is an Agent

An agent is something capable of intelligent behaviour. It could be a robot or a computer program. *Physical agents*, such as robots, have a clear interpretation. They are realized as a physical device that interacts with a physical environment. The majority of AI research, however, is concerned with *virtual* or *software* agents that exist as models occupying a virtual environment held inside a computer.

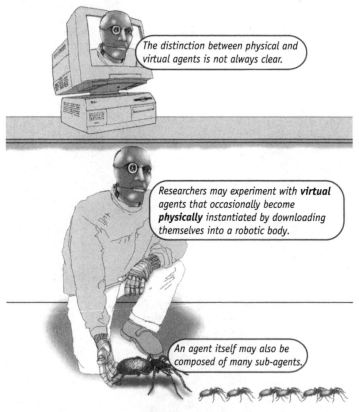

> The distinction between physical and virtual agents is not always clear.

> Researchers may experiment with **virtual** agents that occasionally become **physically** instantiated by downloading themselves into a robotic body.

> An agent itself may also be composed of many sub-agents.

Some AI systems solve problems by employing techniques observed in ant colonies. So, in this case, what appears to be a single agent may be relying on the combined behaviour of hundreds of sub-agents.

AI as an Empirical Science

Artificial Intelligence is a huge undertaking. **Marvin Minsky** (b. 1927), one of the founding fathers of AI, argues: "The AI problem is one of the hardest science has ever undertaken." AI has one foot in science and one in engineering.

*In its most extreme form, known as **Strong AI**, the goal is to build a machine capable of thought, consciousness and emotions. This view holds that humans are no more than elaborate computers.*

Weak AI is less audacious.

The aim of Weak AI is to develop theories of human and animal intelligence, and then test these theories by building working models, usually in the form of computer programs or robots.

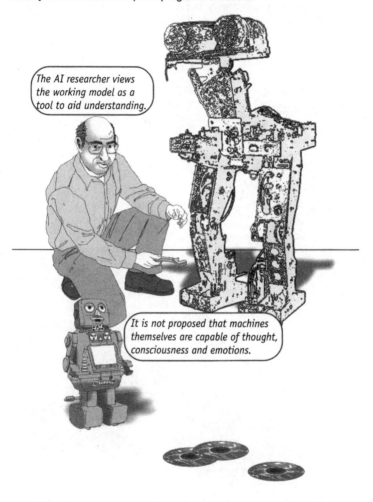

The AI researcher views the working model as a tool to aid understanding.

It is not proposed that machines themselves are capable of thought, consciousness and emotions.

So, for Weak AI, the model is a useful tool for understanding the mind; for Strong AI, the model *is* a mind.

Alien-AI Engineering

AI also aims to build machinery that is not necessarily based on human or animal intelligence.

Such machines may exhibit intelligent behaviour, but the basis for this behaviour is not important.

The aim is to design useful intelligent machinery by whatever means.

Because the mechanisms underlying such systems are not intended to mirror the mechanisms underlying human intelligence, this approach to AI is sometimes termed *Alien-AI*.

Solving the AI Problem

So, for some, solving the AI problem would mean finding a way to build machines with capabilities on a par with, or beyond, those found in humans.

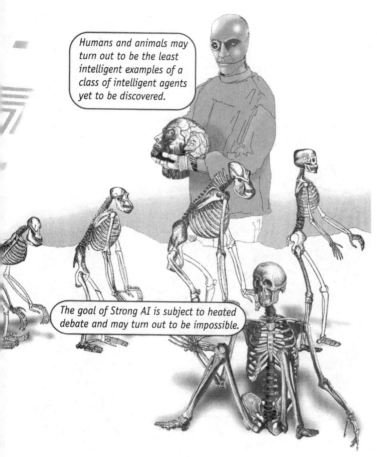

Humans and animals may turn out to be the least intelligent examples of a class of intelligent agents yet to be discovered.

The goal of Strong AI is subject to heated debate and may turn out to be impossible.

But for most researchers working on AI, the outcome of the Strong AI debate is of little direct consequence.

Ambition Within Limits

AI, in its weak form, concerns itself more with the degree to which we can explain the mechanisms that underlie human and animal behaviour.

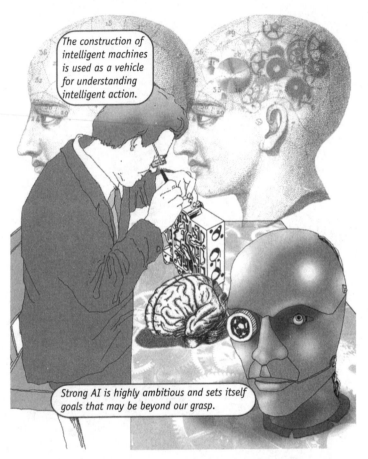

The construction of intelligent machines is used as a vehicle for understanding intelligent action.

Strong AI is highly ambitious and sets itself goals that may be beyond our grasp.

The strong stance can be contrasted with the more widespread and cautious goal of engineering clever machines, which is already an established approach, proven by successful engineering projects.

Taking AI to its Limits

Immortality and Transhumanism

"We cannot hold back AI any more than primitive man could have suppressed the spread of speaking" – Doug Lenat and Edward Feigenbaum

If we assume that Strong AI is a real possibility, then several fundamental questions emerge.

Imagine being able to leave your body and shifting your mental life onto machinery that has better long-term prospects than the constantly ageing organic body you currently inhabit.

*This possibility is entertained by **Transhumanists** and **Extropians**.*

The problem that Strong AI aims to solve must shed light on this possibility. Strong AI's hypothesis is that thought, as well as other mental characteristics, is not inextricably linked to our organic bodies. This makes immortality a possibility, because one's mental life could exist on a more robust platform.

Super-Human Intelligence

Perhaps our intellectual capacity is limited by the design of our brain. Our brain structure has evolved over millions of years. There is absolutely no reason to presume it cannot evolve further, either through continued biological evolution or as a result of human intervention through engineering. The job our brain does is amazing when we consider that the machinery it is made from is very slow in comparison to the cheap electrical components that make up a modern computer.

Neighbouring Disciplines

"Certum quod factum." [One is certain only of what one builds] –
Giambattista Vico (1668–1744)

What sets AI apart from other attempts to understand the mechanisms
behind human and animal cognition is that AI aims to gain
understanding by building working models. Through the synthetic
construction of working models, AI can test and develop theories of
intelligent action.

The big questions of "mental processes" tackled by
AI are bound to a number of disciplines –
psychology, philosophy, linguistics and neuroscience.

AI's goal of constructing
machinery is underpinned
by logic, mathematics and
computer science.

A significant discovery in any one
of these disciplines could impact
on the development of AI.

AI and Psychology

The objectives of AI and psychology overlap. Both aim to understand the mental processes that underpin human and animal behaviour. Psychologists in the late 1950s began to abandon the idea that Behaviourism was the only scientific route to understanding humans.

Pavlov's Dog

*Behaviourists believe that explanations for human and animal behaviour should not appeal to unobserved "mental entities", but rather concentrate on what we can be sure of: **observations of behaviour**.*

Instead of restricting the object of study to stimulus–response relationships, those who abandoned Behaviourism began to consider internal "mentalistic" processes, such as memory, learning and reasoning, as a valid set of concepts for explaining why humans act intelligently.

Cognitive Psychology

Around the same time, the idea that the computer could act as a model of thought was gaining popularity. Putting these two concepts together naturally suggests an approach to psychology based on a computational theory of mind.

In 1957, **Herbert Simon** (1916–2001), an AI pioneer, made the prediction ...

... within 10 years, psychological theories will take the form of computer programs.

By the end of the 1960s, *cognitive psychology* had emerged as a branch of psychology concerned with explaining cognitive function in information-processing terms, and ultimately relying on the computer as a metaphor for cognition.

Cognitive Science

It is clear that AI and cognitive psychology have a great deal of common interest.

AI and Philosophy

Some of the fundamental questions asked by AI have been the hard stuff of philosophers for thousands of years. AI is perhaps unique in the sciences. It has an intimate and reciprocal relationship with philosophy.

In one survey, AI researchers were asked which discipline they felt most closely tied to.

The most frequent answer was **philosophy**.

The Mind-Body Problem

The mind-body problem dates back to **René Descartes** (1596–1650), who argued that there must be a fundamental difference between the mental realm and the physical realm. For Descartes, man was alone in his possession of a mental faculty – animals were mere beasts lacking any mental life.

*But in the case of man, how can the physical body be affected by processes occurring in the **non-physical** mental realm?*

LA MORTE

This is an age-old conundrum …

AI informs modern discussions of the mind-body problem by proposing the *computer metaphor*, which draws a parallel between the relationship of programs to computers and minds to brains.

Computer programs, like minds, have no physical mass yet patently have a causal connection to the physical computer executing the program.

In a similar way, our mind can affect our body.

Computer programs require a computer to manifest themselves – just as a mind requires a brain.

Ontology and Hermeneutics

Attempts to equip machines with knowledge require one to make *ontological assumptions*. Ontology is the branch of philosophy concerned with the kinds of things that exist. AI projects, lasting tens of years, have attempted to distil common-sense knowledge into computers.

To do so, the designers have to decide on the "kind of things" a machine must know in order to make sense of the world.

Insights originating from the branch of continental philosophy known as Hermeneutics have vehemently criticized the very possibility of formalizing mental processes in this way ...

But recently, these criticisms have shaped new approaches to looking at cognition, and have had a positive influence on AI. We will return to this later.

A Positive Start

The term Artificial Intelligence was coined at a small conference at Dartmouth College, New Hampshire, in 1956. Some of its key figures gathered to discuss the following hypothesis ...

Herbert Simon   John McCarthy   Claude Shannon

"Every aspect of learning or any other feature of intelligence can in principle be so precisely described that a machine can be made to simulate it."

Allen Newell   Marvin Minsky

This hypothesis has been subject to intense research ever since. Many of those attending the conference went on to be pivotal in the study of AI.

Optimism and Bold Claims

The Dartmouth conference ran for two months. Two attendants in particular, Allen Newell and Herbert Simon, provoked much discussion by claiming ...

We have invented a computer program capable of thinking non-numerically ...

And thereby solved the venerable mind-body problem.

This was perhaps the first of a long list of bold and enthusiastic claims that litter the history of AI.

AI has always provoked great interest. The possibility of thinking machines has been a mainstay of science fiction. This is partly a result of our fascination with the limits of technology and partly due to enthusiastic AI researchers.

One common criticism of AI is its unashamed self-publicity, as T. Roszak complained in the *New Scientist* in 1986: *"AI's record of barefaced public deception is unparalleled in annals of academic study."*

This statement is still dubious nearly 50 years later. Can machines really think? As we will see later, this is an important question, but it is riddled with conceptual problems. However, a strong case can be made for the existence of machines that *can* learn and create.

Intelligence and Cognition

So what exactly is intelligence, and how do we decide when something is artificial, rather than the real thing? Neither of these questions admits precise definition, which makes Artificial Intelligence an unfortunate name for a branch of science. On the concept of intelligence, A.S. Reber noted in 1995: *"Few concepts in psychology have received more devoted attention and few have resisted classification so thoroughly."*

In the context of AI, intelligent is best taken to mean "exhibiting interesting behaviour".

Interesting behaviour can be found in ants, termites, fish and most other animals ...

But these animals are not considered intelligent in the everyday sense of the word.

Intelligence is the computational part of the ability to achieve goals in the world. Varying kinds and degrees of intelligence occur in people, many animals and some machines.

So there are varying degrees of intelligence, with humans sitting at the "high intelligence" end of the spectrum.

Humans undoubtedly exhibit many interesting behaviours not observed in other organisms – for example, language.

The relationship between behaviour and intelligence is rife with problems. To illustrate these problems, we will consider perhaps the first milestone in autonomous robotics.

Mimicry of Life

During the 1950s in Bristol, south-west England, W. Grey Walter
pioneered the construction of autonomous robots. Walter carried out his
influential work long before the availability of digital computers. He was
interested in *Cybernetics* – the study of the range of possible behaviours
of animals and machines.

Cybernetics rests on the assumption
that the laws that govern the
control of humans, animals and
machines are **universal**.

This means that the same principles can
apply to all three, even though they might
be made from very different materials.

Walter was interested in the "mimicry of life" and built robots that
continue to draw interest today. Using very basic materials, such as
cogs from gas meters, Walter constructed a series of mobile robots that
resembled tortoises.

These robots were autonomous. There was no human intervention or control governing their behaviour. Walter's robots had three wheels and were surrounded by a shell that acted as a bump detector.

As well as detecting collisions with objects, the tortoise also had a light sensor ...

I am designed to be attracted to light.

Using two motors to control the lead wheel, one for steering, and one for propulsion, the robot would seek light. However, when faced with extreme brightness, part of the robot's design made it avoid the source of the light.

Complex Behaviour

Walter reported that one of his creatures, Elsie, exhibited unpredictable behaviour. For example, as part of Elsie's environment, Walter introduced a hutch containing a bright light and a re-charging station.

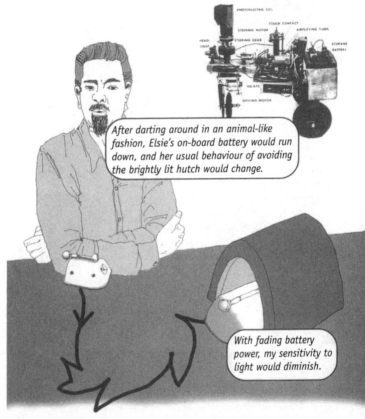

After darting around in an animal-like fashion, Elsie's on-board battery would run down, and her usual behaviour of avoiding the brightly lit hutch would change.

With fading battery power, my sensitivity to light would diminish.

She would now enter what appeared to be a dimly lit hutch and re-charge herself. When full power was restored to the battery, full sensitivity would return, and Elsie would dash out of the hutch and carry on as before.

Is Elsie Intelligent?

Walter's creatures were very simple by modern standards, yet they shed light on issues confronting contemporary robotics by illustrating how complex behaviour can arise from simple machines. There was no way Walter could predict the exact behaviour of his robots.

Elsie's behaviour depends too much on the environment and factors such as fading battery power.

I could certainly achieve goals in the world, since I could sustain my own battery power.

But the capabilities of Elsie are a far cry from what we consider "real" intelligence. Importantly, Elsie has a lot in common with the famous horse known as Clever Hans.

Clever Hans: A Cautionary Tale

Clever Hans was a horse famously taught to do arithmetic by his trainer, Wilhelm von Osten. Hans would tap out the correct answer to a problem with his hoof, to the amazement of the onlooking crowd, and only occasionally make a mistake. Scientific experts supported his trainer's claims: Hans really could do arithmetic. But one expert noticed that Hans was making mistakes when von Osten himself didn't know the answer. Hans's cover was blown.

Making a "Clever Hans error" means mistakenly attributing a capacity to an agent when in fact the capacity is supplied by the environment – in this case, an arithmetically competent human.

Believers of Clever Hans mistakenly ascribed von Osten's intelligence to the horse. Similar criticisms have been levelled at W. Grey Walter's robotic tortoises.

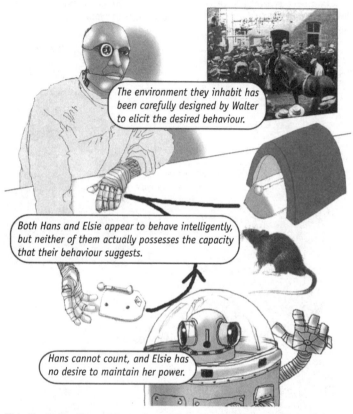

The environment they inhabit has been carefully designed by Walter to elicit the desired behaviour.

Both Hans and Elsie appear to behave intelligently, but neither of them actually possesses the capacity that their behaviour suggests.

Hans cannot count, and Elsie has no desire to maintain her power.

This illustrates the problem of ascribing a capacity to an agent solely on the basis of its behaviour.

How can AI construct intelligent machines, when intelligent action is so intimately related to the environment? The majority of AI research has side-stepped this problem in two ways. First, by focusing on cognition in agents detached from the complexities introduced by real-world environments. Second, AI mainly concerns itself with studying internal cognitive processes, rather than external behaviour.

Language, Cognition and Environment

AI's stance on cognition and environment is exemplified by the linguist and cognitive scientist **Noam Chomsky** (b. 1928). Chomsky's influential insight is that we are born with a strong biological predisposition for language.

I noted that children, wherever they are born, consistently arrive at a complex knowledge of language.

*The **input** for the child is the speech of its parents and other humans.*

*The **output** is an ostensibly complete knowledge of the complex grammatical system underlying my native language.*

On the relationship between these inputs and outputs, Chomsky states:

"An engineer faced with the problem of designing a device for meeting the given input-output conditions would naturally conclude that the basic properties of the output are a consequence of the design of the device. Nor is there any plausible alternative to this assumption, so far as I can see."

Critically, the input the child faces greatly under-specifies the knowledge it ends up with.

I term this phenomenon the **poverty of the stimulus**, and argue that we are **born** with a knowledge of language.

In other words, when considering the human competence for language, the environment plays only a minor role. For Chomsky, language is a cognitive process which is only "partially shaped" by the environment.

Two Strands Concerning the AI Problem

Chomsky's position on language can be taken as the blueprint for the majority of the research into AI over the past 50 years. AI research typically focuses on the high-level processes of *cognition* such as language, memory, learning and reasoning.

> *A prevailing assumption of AI is that these capacities can be understood without considering their messy relationship with a constantly changing and complex environment.*

> *Robotics, however, faces a constant battle with the complexities of real-world environments, and therefore throws up a very different set of problems.*

This book will trace how these two strands have developed over the past half-century. Success for AI, both Strong and Weak, can be approached only when these two strands meet and unify. This must be the case: ultimately, AI seeks working robots with high-level cognitive capacities.

AI's Central Dogma: Cognitivism

Artificial Intelligence rests on the view that cognition is *computational*: the mind and brain are no more than an elaborate computer. This position is known as *cognitivism*.

A cognitivist would claim that all aspects of cognition – mental actions such as learning, memory and even emotions – can be carried out by computing machinery.

To understand this claim, we need a clearer understanding of what is meant by **computation**.

What is Computation?

"I reject all proposals that assume that computation can be defined."
– Brian Cantwell Smith, Indiana University

The notion of computation is at the heart of cognitivism, yet computation is a notoriously hard concept to define. Computation can be simply taken to mean: *"The kind of calculations that computers can perform."*

As a first cut, this definition is adequate.

But this is an empirical claim. It tells us only about the kind of operations that computers, as we know them today, can perform.

Despite the lack of a precise definition, the theory of computation is a well-developed and rigorous branch of computer science that draws heavily on the notion of the *Turing machine*. The British mathematician **Alan Turing** (1912–54) was a crucial pioneer in the history of AI, computer science and logic.

The Turing Machine

One of Turing's achievements was the proposal of a notional computing device: the Turing machine. The Turing machine is a simple imaginary device, part of which is an infinitely long tape on which symbols can be written.

The Turing machine has served an important purpose in the theory of computation. Using his imaginary machine, Turing proved fundamental results that hold true for all known computing devices. Turing achieved this feat before computers, as we know them today, were actually built.

The Brain as a Computing Device

In 1943, aware of Turing's work on computation, **Warren McCulloch** (1898–1968) and **Walter Pitts** (1923–69) published "A Logical Calculus of the Ideas Immanent in Nervous Activity" in which they demonstrate how individual brain neurons can be viewed as computing devices. As a teenager, Walter Pitts used to sneak into classes at the University of Chicago. Impressed by his precocious knowledge of logic, Pitts was invited by the faculty to work with Warren McCulloch, a physiologist.

Together we produced work that revolutionized the science of the brain.

*We explained how small collections of neurons can act as **logic gates** – the building blocks of modern computers.*

and   or   not

Ultimately, they proved that configurations of neurons can perform any calculation computable by a Turing machine. The upshot of this discovery was that brains can be considered as computing devices, just like a Turing machine.

Universal Computation

All computers, however modern, sophisticated or expensive, are restricted. The kind of calculations that they can perform are *precisely* those that can be calculated by a Turing machine. This observation means that we only need to consider Turing machines when analysing what is and what is not computable. All other machines, including brains, can be reduced to the Turing machine.

The class of calculations that either can perform turns out to be identical to those computable by a Turing machine.

*These results are evidence for treating the Turing machine as a **model of universal computation**.*

Any calculation your computer or your brain can perform, Turing's 65-year-old imaginary computer can do too.

Computation and Cognitivism

Although all computing devices can be considered identical to a Turing machine in the class of calculations they can compute, the manners in which these different devices perform the calculations differ in fundamental ways.

The Turing machine reads and writes symbols onto an imaginary tape ...

A typical desktop computer performs operations on a random access memory ...

And the brain computes using a vast network of neurons.

So when we talk of computation in terms of the class of calculations computers can perform, this tells us little more than *what* these calculations can achieve, rather than *how*. Which model of computation is cognitivism proposing? How exactly does the mind compute?

The Machine Brain

Throughout history, scientists have claimed that the activity going on inside our heads is mechanical. During the Renaissance, it was thought that this mechanical activity resembled a clockwork device, and later on, a steam engine. Within the last century, the metaphor of a telephone exchange was invoked.

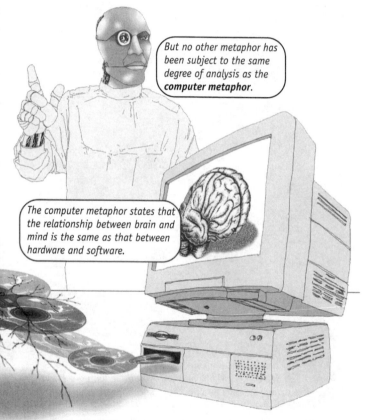

*But no other metaphor has been subject to the same degree of analysis as the **computer metaphor**.*

The computer metaphor states that the relationship between brain and mind is the same as that between hardware and software.

The brain is like the hardware: it is a physical device. The mind is like the software: it requires the physical device to operate, but in itself it is not material since it has no mass.

Functionalist Separation of Mind from Brain

Functionalism is the idea that the kind of operations that define a computation are what matters, rather than the nature of their physical instantiation. So long as two processes carry out the same function, they can be considered identical. So functionalism means *multiple realization*, because the same operation can be realized physically in many different ways.

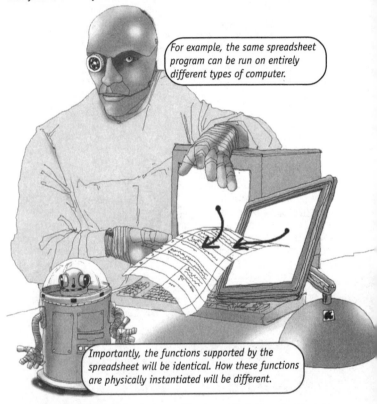

For example, the same spreadsheet program can be run on entirely different types of computer.

Importantly, the functions supported by the spreadsheet will be identical. How these functions are physically instantiated will be different.

A functionalist would claim that cognition is not tied down to any one kind of machinery. What is special about the mind is the kind of operations it carries out, rather than the fact that it is physically supported by a brain made up of millions of neurons.

The Physical Symbol Systems Hypothesis

In 1976, Newell and Simon proposed the *Physical Symbol Systems Hypothesis* (PSSH). This hypothesis proposes a set of properties that characterize the kind of computations that the mind relies on. The PSSH states that intelligent action must rely on the syntactic manipulation of symbols: *"A physical symbol system has the necessary and sufficient means for intelligent action."* Which is to say that cognition requires the manipulation of symbolic representations, and these representations refer to things in the world.

> The system must be physically realized, but the "stuff" the system is built from is irrelevant.

> So it could be made of neurons, silicon, or even tin cans.

In essence, Newell and Simon are commenting on the kind of *program* that the computer runs – they say nothing about the kind of computer that runs the program.

A Theory of Intelligent Action

Newell and Simon's hypothesis is an attempt to clarify the issue of the kind of operations that are required for intelligent action. However, the PSSH is only a hypothesis, and so must be tested. Its validity as a hypothesis can only be proved or disproved by scientists carrying out experiments. Traditionally, AI is the science of testing this hypothesis.

Recall that the PSSH makes a claim about the kind of program that the brain supports.

And so, arriving at the **right program** is all that is required for a theory of intelligent action.

Importantly, they take a functionalist stance – the nature of the machinery that supports this program is not the principal concern.

Could a Machine *Really* Think?

Let's examine the claim of the cognitivists. Imagine they have been successful: they have realized the goal of Strong AI, and constructed an intelligent, thinking machine. Do we believe them? Is cognitivism fundamentally naïve? Perhaps there is a decisive argument that proves machines cannot think.

Alan Turing, in his seminal 1950 paper, "Computing Machinery and Intelligence", was interested in the question "Can machines think?" Turing recognized that the question was ill-defined and "too meaningless to deserve discussion".

*I replaced the question with the **imitation game**.*

The imitation game requires a human interrogator to decide whether the agent at the end of a text-based computer link is either a computer or a human.

Both parties are in different rooms ...

The Turing Test

The interrogator can ask any question he or she chooses, and on the basis of the responses, which don't necessarily have to be truthful, must decide on either humanoid or computer. Turing imagined the following kind of dialogue.

If the computer can fool the human interrogator into believing it is human, it passes the Turing test.

Turing's problem with the question "Can machines think?" is a problem with the term "think". What exactly is thought? How do we decide when it is going on? Adopting everyday usage of the word would relegate the question, according to Turing, to a statistical survey like a Gallup poll.

This is not how we want to decide if a machine thinks or not.

Noam Chomsky, too, has a problem with the question.

I liken the question to asking "Can submarines swim?"

Any answer is little about fact, and more about "sharpening our usage" of words like "think" and "swim".

The Loebner Prize

In 1990 the Turing test was turned into an annual competition. Every year contestants compete for the Loebner prize. The first person to design a computer program that passes the Turing test gets $100,000 and a gold medal. No one has managed to claim the gold medal yet, but bronze medals and cash are given out to the best efforts every year. Here is an excerpt from conversation between a judge and a computer:

It is unlikely that any computer will pass the Turing test in the near future.

Problems with the Turing Test

Many object to Turing's imitation game as a test for intelligence or thought. The principal objection is that the test only takes into account the linguistic behaviour of the machine. It ignores *how* the machine operates.

"The fundamental goal of this research is not merely to mimic intelligence or produce some clever fake. Not at all. 'AI' wants only the genuine article: machines with minds, in the full and literal sense."
– John Haugeland

Imagine a machine that passes the Turing test, but does so by patently non-intelligent means.

For example, as a thought experiment, imagine a machine that could memorize all possible conversational fragments up to a given length.

Hello... my name is Roddy...

let me think about that...

Then, through verbatim regurgitation, such a machine might pass the test.

you may be right but... the way I see things...

Although in practice this is likely to be impossible, some have used it as an illustration of the inadequacy of the Turing test.

Inside the Machine: Searle's Chinese Room

In the 1980s, the philosopher John Searle, frustrated with the claims made by AI researchers that their machines had "understanding" of the structures they manipulate, devised a thought experiment in an attempt to deal a knockout-blow to those touting Strong AI.

In contrast to the Turing test, my argument revolves around the nature of the computations going on **inside** the computer.

Searle attempts to show that purely syntactic symbol manipulation, like that proposed by Newell and Simon's PSSH, cannot by itself lead to a machine thinking or understanding.

Searle's Chinese Room

Searle imagined himself inside a room. One side of the room has a hatch through which questions, written in Chinese, are passed in to Searle. His job is to provide answers, also in Chinese, to these questions. The answers are passed back outside the room through another hatch. The problem is, Searle does not understand a word of Chinese, and Chinese characters mean nothing to him.

To help construct the answers to the questions, I am armed with a set of complex rule-books which tell me how to manipulate the meaningless Chinese symbols into an answer to the question.

With enough practice, Searle gets very skilled at constructing the answers. To the outside world, Searle's behaviour does not differ from that of a native Chinese speaker – the Chinese room passes the Turing test.

Unlike a genuine literate in Chinese, Searle does not in any way understand the symbols he is manipulating. Similarly, a computer executing the same procedure – the manipulation of abstract symbols – would have no understanding of the Chinese symbols either.

I have everything that Newell and Simon's physical symbol systems hypothesis asks for – and yet I do not understand Chinese.

The crux of Searle's argument is that **whatever** formal principles are given to the computer, they will not be sufficient for understanding ...

Because even when a human carries out the manipulation of these symbols, they will still understand absolutely nothing.

Searle's conclusion is that formal symbol manipulation is not enough to account for understanding. This conclusion is in direct conflict with Newell and Simon's physical symbol systems hypothesis.

One Answer to Searle

One frequent retort to Searle's argument is that Searle himself might not understand Chinese, but the combination of Searle and the rule-book *do* understand Chinese.

I dismiss this point by arguing that a combination of constituents without understanding cannot magically invoke understanding.

Here, Searle is arguing that the whole cannot be more than the sum of its parts.

For many, this point is a weakness in Searle's argument.

Can the whole be more than the sum of its parts? There is sound evidence that a "combination of constituents" does indeed result in a higher order of complexity, a "greater whole".

Applying Complexity Theory

Complexity, the science of understanding order arising from complex interactions of simple constituents, deals in the possibility of *emergence*. Emergent properties are those that cannot be predicted simply through an understanding of constituent behaviours.

*Complex interactions between simple parts can lead to what is called **self-organization**.*

Self-organization occurs when high-level properties emerge from the interaction of simple components.

Let's consider an example of emergence in biology ...

Is Understanding an Emergent Property?

Humans emerge from the human genome, which massively under-specifies precisely how to build a human. Of course, we are the product of our genes, but only in combination with an immensely complex interaction between our genes, the polypeptide chains they produce, and how these chains go on to interact.

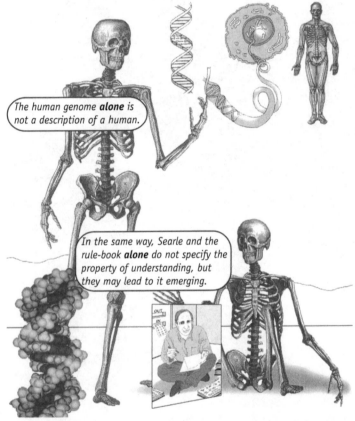

> The human genome **alone** is not a description of a human.

> In the same way, Searle and the rule-book **alone** do not specify the property of understanding, but they may lead to it emerging.

In a nutshell, complexity theory tells us that the whole can be more than the sum of its parts, although this argument by itself does not constitute an explanation of the emergence of understanding.

Machines Built From the Right Stuff

It is important to note that Searle is not denying the possibility of Strong AI. Indeed, Searle believes that we are nothing more than complex machines, and therefore we *can* build machines that think and understand. Searle's objection is with the notion that machine understanding is simply a matter of coming up with the *right program*. Searle strikes at the heart of functionalism.

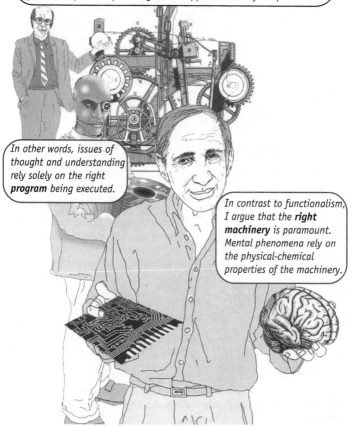

The functionalist argument assumes that the nature of the machinery is of no consequence – providing it can support the act of computation.

*In other words, issues of thought and understanding rely solely on the right **program** being executed.*

*In contrast to functionalism, I argue that the **right machinery** is paramount. Mental phenomena rely on the physical-chemical properties of the machinery.*

AI and Dualism

For Searle, to argue anything else means you must believe in a form of *dualism*, the position that the mental realm has no causal connection with the physical realm. According to Searle, this is precisely the position many AI researchers take. They believe that their models have a mental life purely on the basis of the right program being executed. Mental phenomena can be understood solely in terms of programs (mind), independent of machinery (brain).

This is a provocative charge, as few scientists would be happy to admit to the existence of a non-physical mental realm.

In short, computers, as we know them today, are not made of the right stuff to support thinking, understanding, and consciousness.

He believes that pursuing AI by seeking the "right program" is misguided. Qualities such as understanding require the right kind of machinery as well.

The Brain Prosthesis Experiment

The roboticist **Hans Moravec** (b. 1948) proposed *The Brain Prosthesis Experiment* which clearly illustrates the divided opinions on where properties such as thought, understanding, and consciousness reside. Imagine replacing the neurons in your brain, one at a time, with electronic substitute neurons – gradually transforming your brain from a biological device into an electronic one. Assuming we have a complete understanding of the behaviour of neurons, and our artificial neurons mimic this behaviour under all possible conditions, the behaviour of the transformed brain will be identical to that of the biological brain.

Roger Penrose and Quantum Effects

For Searle, the nature of the machinery required for consciousness is a mystery. He makes no claim to have an answer explaining why computers cannot support properties such as understanding and consciousness, but brains can. In contrast, Roger Penrose, a mathematical physicist at the University of Oxford, proposes a candidate "stuff".

Like Searle, Penrose argues that conventional computing machinery cannot support consciousness. A conscious mind requires very specific physical characteristics.

I accept that mentality must arise from physicality.

But I believe that a new kind of physics is required to explain conscious thought.

If Penrose is correct, then this poses a problem for AI ...

Computers are inherently limited in the kind of processes they can support.

Penrose and Gödel's Theorem

To support his argument, Penrose appeals to a fundamental theorem in mathematical logic – Gödel's Theorem – which states that certain mathematical truths cannot be proved by using a computational procedure. Because human mathematicians evidently can arrive at these truths, Penrose claims that humans must be performing *non-computable operations*.

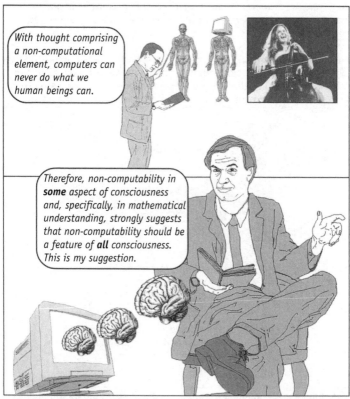

With thought comprising a non-computational element, computers can never do what we human beings can.

*Therefore, non-computability in **some** aspect of consciousness and, specifically, in mathematical understanding, strongly suggests that non-computability should be a feature of **all** consciousness. This is my suggestion.*

If human thought comprises non-computational processes, then how is the brain supporting these processes? To answer this question, Penrose appeals to physics, and claims that the theory of **quantum gravity** is likely to be the kind of physics required to explain a conscious mind.

Quantum Gravity and Consciousness

The theory of quantum gravity, which is still at a very tentative stage, is targeted to account for the measurable inaccuracies we observe using current physics. That is, neither quantum theory nor relativity theory can comprehensively explain certain small-scale phenomena. Penrose states: *"This new theory will not just be a slight modification of quantum mechanics but something as different from standard quantum mechanics as General Relativity is different from Newtonian gravity. It would have to be something which has a completely different conceptual framework."*

The idea that quantum gravity may prove important to our understanding of consciousness predates Penrose, but he has stuck his neck out and specifically proposed that *quantum gravity effects* in the brain are likely to rely on **microtubules** – conveyor-belt-like structures inside neurons.

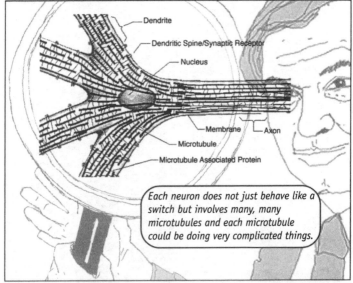

Dendrite

Dendritic Spine/Synaptic Receptor

Nucleus

Membrane — Axon

Microtubule

Microtubule Associated Protein

Each neuron does not just behave like a switch but involves many, many microtubules and each microtubule could be doing very complicated things.

Microtubules, according to Penrose, support a substrate for the quantum gravity effects required for consciousness. Crucially, these processes are non-computable – they cannot be supported by conventional computing machinery. This speculative proposal supports Penrose's assertion that human thought relies on non-computable processes.

Because computers, as we know them today, do not have a cellular structure comprising microtubules, they cannot support consciousness. Penrose may well be right, but there is as yet scant evidence to support his claim. The idea that there is some hitherto unconsidered ingredient missing from our classical understanding of biological systems is a common conclusion to debates regarding the possibility of conscious thinking machines. Penrose's theory is very controversial and few accept his conclusions.

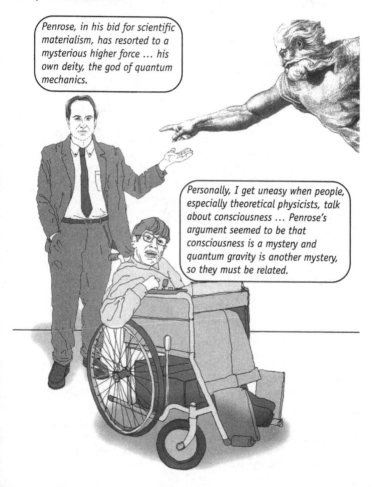

Penrose, in his bid for scientific materialism, has resorted to a mysterious higher force ... his own deity, the god of quantum mechanics.

Personally, I get uneasy when people, especially theoretical physicists, talk about consciousness ... Penrose's argument seemed to be that consciousness is a mystery and quantum gravity is another mystery, so they must be related.

Is AI Really About Thinking Machines?

Understanding, Consciousness and Thought are a Mystery.

Given our current understanding, there really is no answer to the question of mechanized understanding, consciousness or thought. This debate is best reduced to the issue of intentionality, one that philosophers have been struggling with since medieval times.

*The term intentionality, when used by philosophers, refers to the **aboutness** of things.*

Mental states have aboutness – for example, beliefs and desires – and it requires a conscious mind to have these intentional states.

*Consciousness is always **of** something, including consciousness **of** itself ...*

Edmund Husserl (1859–1938), founder of phenomenology

Franz Brentano (1837–1917), psychologist and philosopher

AI has stumbled upon this age-old problem. What exactly is intentionality, does it really exist, and if so, does it have a physical basis? Unfortunately, the intentionality debate remains a mystery, irrespective of the claims made by some AI researchers that their machines can think and understand.

Tackling the Intentionality Problem

The kind of machinery used by AI researchers, and how this machinery sheds light on the question of intentionality, are problems rarely considered by those carrying out active research into AI. Practical research proceeds independent of this debate. Most AI researchers agree that we can investigate theories of intelligent behaviour, and implement these theories as computer models, without the need to account for intentionality.

A typical AI researcher writes computer programs on standard computers.

Similarly, roboticists do not try to attack the question of intentionality by using certain kinds of machinery.

Addressing the issue of intentionality is implicitly regarded by those working in AI as part of the "finishing touches". First, they aim to get computers and robots to behave intelligently, and only then will these fundamental questions be taken on.

Investigating the Cognitivist Stance

The classical approach to AI encompasses a set of principles and practices used to explore the validity of cognitivism, and specifically, to investigate the hypothesis proposed by Newell and Simon. Cognition is best understood as the formal manipulation of symbolic structures.

The classical approach to AI has resulted in engineering projects such as the following, which we shall examine in more detail later.

- Chess-playing computers capable of beating the best human players.

- Attempts to equip computers with common-sense knowledge.

- Computer vision systems capable of recovering information about objects in a scene captured by a camera.

- Shakey, a robot capable of carrying out tasks using several AI technologies, such as vision, planning, and natural language processing.

Sense-Think-Act

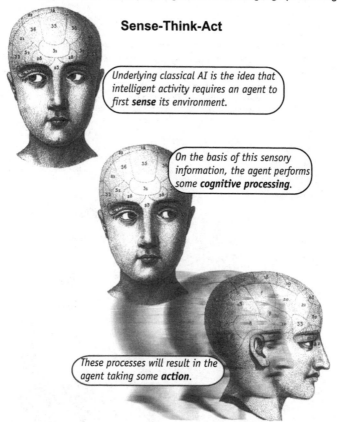

Underlying classical AI is the idea that intelligent activity requires an agent to first **sense** its environment.

On the basis of this sensory information, the agent performs some **cognitive processing**.

These processes will result in the agent taking some **action**.

In short, the connection between perception and action is mediated by the act of cognition.

Beyond Elsie

As we will see, the robot Shakey has cognitive capacities well beyond those found in W. Grey Walter's robotic tortoise, Elsie. Recall what Elsie was lacking …

- She did not have knowledge of where she was or where she was going.
- She was not programmed to achieve any goals.
- She had little or no cognitive capacity.

Elsie lacked the very capacities that classical AI seeks to understand: cognitive abilities such as reasoning, learning, vision and understanding language.

In contrast to Elsie, Shakey stands as a prime example of a cognitive robot.

Shakey relies on a number of AI technologies. But before Shakey could be built, researchers had to consider Shakey's constituent parts.

Cognitive Modelling

Much of AI hinges on *cognitive modelling*. This means the construction of computer models which carry out some cognitive function.

The manner in which these models achieve the task may mirror a theory of human cognition.

Alternatively, the cognitive model might encapsulate an entirely new way of solving the problem, using methods not found in nature.

But the problem has not been solved. The construction of a working model does not by itself constitute an *explanation* for the thing being modelled.

A Model Is Not an Explanation

Imagine someone handing you a wiring diagram of the human brain – a total map of the brain's neural structure. Using this wiring diagram, you might then go and build a mechanical brain.

Imagine that the result is a machine capable of learning, reasoning and other cognitive capacities.

Now, have you really got a satisfactory explanation of human cognition?

For example, would the model help us to understand cognitive processes such as the relationship between long- and short-term memory? The problem is, we might have a working model, yet not understand the model in the way we would like.

The Nematode

In fact, we have such a wiring diagram of the whole nervous system of a nematode called *Caenorhabditis elegans*. The biology of this worm is remarkably well understood. In 2002, Sydney Brenner, H. Robert Horvitz and John E. Sulston won the Nobel Prize in Physiology for their work uncovering precisely how the fully mature worm (about a millimetre long) develops from its DNA.

Because the worm is transparent, every one of the 959 cells that make up a mature worm can be traced from the conception of a single cell.

Some of these cells – neurons – make up the worm's brain, while others are used to construct cellular structures such as sense organs and muscles.

John Sulston

Really Understanding Behaviour

These recent advances in understanding *Caenorhabditis elegans* are fundamental to biology. The developmental path from a single cell to a mature organism involves a massively complex series of interactions.

Caenorhabditis elegans is simple enough for us to obtain a detailed map of its cellular structure.

*But even though this worm is very well understood at the neural level, the manner in which the neural structures are **configured to yield behaviour** is hardly understood at all.*

So, even if we decided to build the nematode on the basis of the wiring diagram, there would still be a huge gap in our understanding of the control mechanisms underlying the behaviour of *Caenorhabditis elegans*.

Reducing the Level of Description

One of the problems with an explanation based on a detailed wiring diagram is that the level of description is too fine-grained to be useful. But what is the appropriate conceptual vocabulary for explaining cognitive processes? Classical AI, in exploring Newell and Simon's hypothesis, aims to explain cognition in terms of a computer program manipulating symbolic representations.

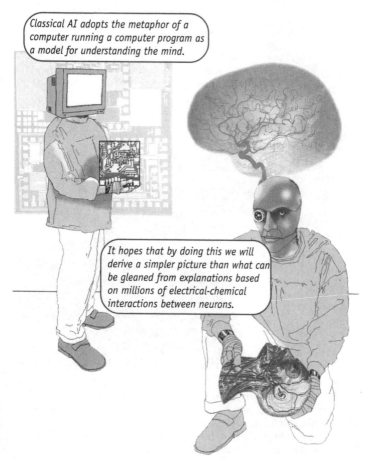

Classical AI adopts the metaphor of a computer running a computer program as a model for understanding the mind.

It hopes that by doing this we will derive a simpler picture than what can be gleaned from explanations based on millions of electrical-chemical interactions between neurons.

Simplifying the Problem

The enthusiasm evident in early AI research was tempered by the realization that, in fact, the problem is exceptionally hard. For example, it was thought initially, during the 1950s, that machine translation would be an unproblematic and viable proposition.

Automatic machine translation from, say, Russian to English would largely be a matter of constructing the appropriate mechanical dictionaries.

Researchers soon found this not to be the case.

In 1963, after spending $20 million on research into machine translation, the US funding agency concluded: "There is no immediate or predictable prospect of useful machine translation" – National Academy of Sciences National Research Council, 1963.

Faced with a hard problem, AI research will often begin by simplifying it. Two kinds of simplification are frequently made.

Decompose and Simplify

Fortunately, cognitive brain functions are not part of a complex mush that cannot be decomposed. Many have argued that our brain is structured rather like an interconnected set of sub-computers. Some of these sub-computers seem to work independently, which is good news for AI. The psychologist Jerry Fodor, in the 1980s, proposed that the mind is largely composed of a set of task-specific modules.

Sensory data is transformed when it passes through these modules, and each module encapsulates the solution to a specific task.

Importantly, many of these modules cannot read the contents of other modules – they are autonomous systems.

Consider the Muller-Lyer illusion. Line 1 and Line 2 are of the same length, although Line 2 appears to be longer than Line 1. Even though we have knowledge that tells us the two lines are of equal length, our perception of the two arrows is not privy to this information. Our perception "module" must be working independently of this knowledge.

The Module Basis

So if we assume the modularity of mind, then by taking on each module and attempting to understand it to a degree that it can be built, progress towards AI's goal of understanding and building cognitive capacities can proceed on a module by module basis. Instead of unleashing a model of cognition into the real, unwashed world, it is far simpler to construct a simplified virtual world. A *micro-world* is such a simplified virtual world.

Micro-worlds aim to capture the relevant parts of the vastly more complex real world.

By abstracting away from the gory details that make the real world so complex, micro-worlds make building models easier.

The Micro-World

The quintessential micro-world is *blocks world* – a three-dimensional world composed of coloured blocks, pyramids, and other geometric solids.

Other AI programs operate within a virtual blocks world – the world as modelled by the computer itself. By building a machine capable of operating in a micro-world, the hope is that the same kind of machine can be generalized to work in more complex environments.

Early Successes: Game Playing

Games like checkers (draughts) and chess provide the ideal working environment for an AI program. The kind of competence required to play these games is extremely specialized. The micro-worlds that games present are ones of strict rules, uncomplicated environments and predictable consequences. AI thrives on these properties, and as a result, game-playing machines are very successful.

The first chess program to play a whole game against a human was designed by Alan Turing in 1951.

Soon after, **Arthur Samuel** (1901–90) designed a checkers-playing program.

It soon started to beat me regularly.

Self-Improving Program

As a result of learning from its experience, the program carried on improving quickly and soon beat a checkers champion. The champion remarked after defeat in 1965 ...

> *In the matter of the end game, I have not had such competition from any human being since 1954, when I lost my last game.*

This victory of machine over man is widely cited, and for good reason. It demonstrates an important lesson: the capabilities of an artificial agent are not necessarily restricted by the capabilities of the designer. Samuel's program plays better checkers than he does.

Representing the Game Internally

Most game-playing machines work by constructing a symbolic representation called a *game tree*. From the starting position, the game tree details all the possible ways the game can unfold. The representation is symbolic: it might use a symbol to represent a white piece, and another symbol to represent a black piece.

Using these basic symbols, along with a representation of the board, we can represent board positions inside the computer.

For example, here is part of the game tree for tic-tac-toe (noughts and crosses).

Position 1

1st move (human)

2nd move (computer)

3rd move (human)

Two possible paths through the tree are shown. These two paths represent two possible games.

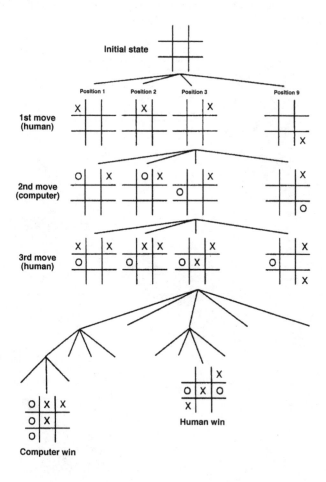

Unlike a human, a computer can easily generate the game tree and keep it in memory. Using this internal representation, the computer can then look ahead to see the precise consequences of its actions.

Brute Force "Search Space" Exploration

Tic-tac-toe is not very demanding. Most people soon realize that they can guarantee at least a draw by employing a simple strategy.

Similarly, designing a computer program to achieve this level of competence is easy because tic-tac-toe has a relatively small game tree – it comprises only 362,880 possible board positions.

By generating the entire game tree, the computer can always make the right decision by looking ahead. It can guarantee a win or a draw. The element of surprise is removed, once you can see how all the possible games unfold.

Infinite Chess Spaces

The space of all possible tic-tac-toe games is negligible in comparison to the number of possible games of chess. One of the world's greatest chess masters, Garry Kasparov, perfectly expressed the difficulty.

The number of potential chess moves exceeds the number of atoms in the universe. It's a number beyond any possible calculation.

With chess, looking ahead even a moderate number of moves becomes intractable – the number of combinations becomes too large to contemplate. The game tree for chess cannot fit into the universe, let alone a computer's memory.

Getting By With Heuristics

In chess, winning board positions are situated deep in the game tree. Chess-playing computers cannot reach these positions by search. It would take too long. Instead, they look ahead only a certain distance. Using a measure which reflects how advantageous a given board position is, these intermediate positions are ranked, and the best one is chosen.

Ranking is achieved by assigning a score to each board position ...

*The score, calculated using an **evaluation function**, reflects how good the position is by taking into account tactical knowledge – like the fact that losing a piece is a bad idea – as well as higher-level tactical strategy.*

These tactical rules of thumb are called *heuristics* and crop up in AI systems everywhere. Heuristics don't guarantee success or correctness, but offer a good approximation. Heuristics are used when more exhaustive and precise methods are intractable.

Deep Blue

Perhaps the most legendary victory of machine over man occurred in 1987. IBM's tailor-made chess computer *Deep Blue* defeated Garry Kasparov, the most highly ranked player in the world. This was a landmark for AI.

The AI community had designed a machine that could beat a highly skilled and dedicated human at a task most people consider to require intelligence.

But does Deep Blue's victory over Kasparov really constitute a significant milestone for AI?

"Deep Blue is stunningly effective at solving chess problems, but it is less 'intelligent' than even the stupidest human." – The IBM Deep Blue website.

Lack of Progress

Chess-playing computers shed little light on the question of mechanized cognition. They unashamedly rely on the ability of machines to consider hundreds of millions of moves per second. Kasparov can only examine a maximum of three moves per second. Deep Blue won using brute force, not brains.

*By citing Deep Blue as one of AI's few examples of success, some within AI itself view this as a reflection of AI's **lack** of progress.*

Deep Blue patently relies on mechanical trickery rather than mental dexterity.

Touting Deep Blue as a success amounts to AI putting its hands up and admitting lack of progress in replicating anything even approaching human cognition.

Giving Machines Knowledge

Our world is more like chess than tic-tac-toe. We can never plan too far ahead; the number of possibilities available to us in our everyday life is too great to contemplate.

Chess-playing machines rely on knowledge coded into their evaluation functions ...

Just as we have knowledge to help us function in a complex environment.

Logic and Thought

The idea that knowledge can be formalized is not new. For centuries the act of thinking has been seen as calculation based on logical reasoning. Newell and Simon's physical symbol systems hypothesis has its roots in the work of the philosopher **Thomas Hobbes** (1588–1679).

Hobbes argued that thought was merely the syntactic manipulation of basic atomic units ...

And these, when put together, could describe the rich structures required for knowledge and thought.

When man reasons, he does nothing else but conceive a sum total from addition of parcels.

Hobbes's "parcels" were the basic units of thought, just as symbols are basic to Newell and Simon's Physical Symbol Systems Hypothesis.

Hobbes's ideas were furthered by the mathematician and philosopher **Gottfried Wilhelm Leibniz** (1646–1716) who tried to identify an appropriate system of parcels – a logical language. Leibniz imagined writing down all the facts known to man in this language, which he called *Characteristica Universalis*.

Then, through calculation, Leibniz believed he would be able to solve any problem.

$$\frac{1}{2}\sin x \cos x \leq \frac{x}{2} \leq \frac{1}{2}\tan x$$

Even moral debates could then be resolved through sheer calculation.

Once the characteristic numbers [atoms] are established for most concepts, mankind will then possess a new instrument which will enhance the capabilities of the mind to far greater extent than optical instruments strengthen the eyes, and will supersede the microscope and telescope to the same extent that reason is superior to eyesight.

Logical reasoning requires the manipulation of sentences described in a logical language. These sentences can be interpreted as representing concepts such as states of affairs in the world – or knowledge. Using computers to automate this process, AI has taken the "logic as thought" idea and built on it.

The CYC Project and Brittleness

Although many thinkers have explored the relationship between logic and thought, few have translated their ideas into an engineering project as bold as Doug Lenat, AI researcher, and head of the CYC project. The CYC project (from en**cyc**lopaedia), started in 1984, is unparalleled in its goal of endowing machines with commonsense knowledge. Lenat describes this project as "mankind's first foray into large-scale ontological engineering". Millions of dollars have been spent on this 20-year project to collect over 100 million facts.

It is relatively easy to equip AI systems with specialized knowledge.

Yet, even a slight deviation from the machine's narrow expertise will inevitably come up with nonsense. This is known as **brittleness** …

Ask a medical program about a rusty old car, and it might blithely diagnose measles.

The aim of CYC is to alleviate the problem of brittleness by codifying the background of commonsense knowledge that we all share. On the difficulty of this task, Lenat notes ...

Many of the prerequisite skills and assumptions have become implicit through millennia of cultural and biological evolution and through universal early childhood experiences.

Before machines can share knowledge as flexibly as people do, those prerequisites need to be recapitulated somehow in explicit, computable forms.

Some have drawn a parallel between Lenat's project and that of Leibniz. Can a large part of our conception of the world really be captured in some formal logical language? As we will see later, the idea that our implicit knowledge of the world can be formalized at all is controversial.

Can the CYC Project Succeed?

The CYC project is entering its final phase, with Lenat predicting a 50% chance of success. Apart from the practical benefits of a successful CYC project, the theoretical objective is to test Newell and Simon's hypothesis. Is commonsense something that we can formalize and automate using symbolic representations?

A recurring justification for the inadequacy of logic-based systems is the "just one more rule" defence. Rather than questioning the enterprise as a whole, the tendency is to persevere with the powerful idea of formalized knowledge dating back to Hobbes.

A Cognitive Robot: Shakey

Shakey, an autonomous mobile robot, is the classic example of how multiple AI techniques can be successfully combined. In contrast to Elsie, Shakey has a lot going on inside. He was the first robot to be controlled by a computer. Built at the Stanford Research Institute in the late 1960s, Shakey is about the size of a fridge and moves around on small wheels.

I navigate with the aid of an optical range-finder, bump detectors, but primarily by using a television camera.

Due to the weight of his hardware, Shakey tends to shake when moved. Hence his name.

Shakey's Environment

Shakey occupied a simplified environment composed of a suite of rooms connected by a corridor. The rooms were bare and contained box-like objects.

Because the environment was constrained, Shakey could reliably work out the location of blocks using a machine vision system.

Sense-Model-Plan-Act

Shakey's design mirrors the traditional view that an agent should be decomposed into four functional components. This model revolves around the *sense-model-plan-act* cycle. First, the agent senses the world. Then a model of the world is constructed on the basis of the sensory inputs. Using this model, a plan can then be constructed to guide how the agent will carry out actions in the world.

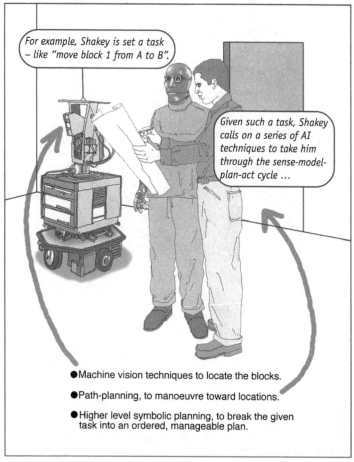

For example, Shakey is set a task – like "move block 1 from A to B".

Given such a task, Shakey calls on a series of AI techniques to take him through the sense-model-plan-act cycle ...

- Machine vision techniques to locate the blocks.
- Path-planning, to manoeuvre toward locations.
- Higher level symbolic planning, to break the given task into an ordered, manageable plan.

Limited to Plan

By shunting the blocks around according to the plan, Shakey can complete the goal set for him. For example, the plan might require the placement of a wedge, acting as a ramp, in order to move one block located on top of another. Due to his weight, Shakey's wheels tended to slip, and as a result, he became inaccurate when navigating.

The planning design was monolithic. After the plan was set into action, Shakey largely ignored feedback from the real world. For example, if someone secretly removed the block Shakey was interested in, he would become very confused.

New Shakey

Efforts to alleviate Shakey's problems led to refinements. Lower level monitoring of movement was introduced to achieve more accurate synchronization.

Whenever inaccuracies were likely, the system made sure the representations and plans were true to the environment by re-checking Shakey's location.

Shakey's Limitations

The integration of many subsystems, not originally designed with Shakey in mind, was an impressive feat. The whole cycle, from perception to modelling, planning and execution, and finally to error recovery, had not been done to this level before.

Perhaps of more significance, the limitations of Shakey taught roboticists valuable lessons.

First, my underlying technology depended heavily on the fact that the environment was simplified.

The machine vision system knew what to expect, and the planning system only had to deal with the movement of blocks.

Given a more complex environment, Shakey's techniques would not cope.

Shakey was also in some ways too clever. He was doing too much.

Often, I would stall for minutes while computing plans and constructing routes.

Given that Shakey's world was kept simple, these problems would multiply when faced with a more complex environment.

The Connectionist Stance

Using the metaphor of a computer executing a program, classical AI seeks to explain cognition in terms of the manipulation of symbolic representations. The mind manipulates symbolic representations in the same way that a program manipulates data.

*This vocabulary of explanation, according to our physical symbol systems hypothesis, is **required** for explaining the basis for intelligent action.*

axons (connections)

neurons (units)

***Connectionism**, an approach inspired by the neural structure of human and animal brains, offers an alternative vocabulary of explanation.*

Connectionism gained popularity in the 1980s and is often depicted as a radical departure from the classical, symbolic approach to AI. Rather than viewing the processes of the mind as a computer program, connectionism draws a parallel between the processes of the mind and the processes of the brain.

Biological Influences

If we look at the biological systems that support cognition, we see brains of varying sizes built from collections of *neurons*.

Neurons are brain cells capable of sending signals to other neurons.

The human brain has approximately 100 billion neurons, and on average, each one of those neurons is connected to around 10,000 other neurons by cable-like structures called *axons*.

Neural Computation

As we saw before, collections of neurons can act as computing devices, and the work of McCulloch and Pitts tells us that these configurations of neurons can compute the same class of calculations as a Turing machine.

Neural Networks

Connectionist models usually take the form of *artificial neural networks*, referred to as *neural networks*. Neural networks are groups of artificial neurons configured to perform some calculation. Neural networks are becoming increasingly well known.

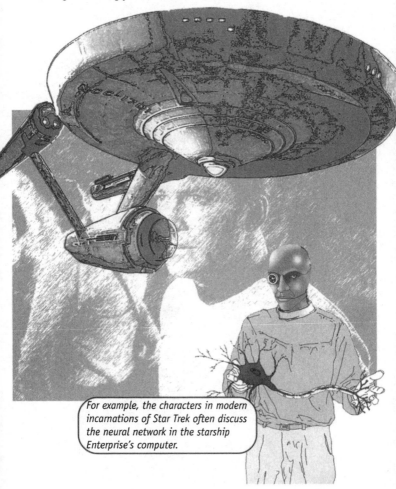

For example, the characters in modern incarnations of Star Trek often discuss the neural network in the starship Enterprise's computer.

The Anatomy of a Neural Network

The building blocks of neural networks are simplified versions of biological neurons called *activation units*. These units have a set of input connections and a set of output connections. These connections model the job performed by axons.

The input connections deliver the signals sent from other neurons.

Depending on the combined strength of all the input signals, the activation unit will send a signal to all the units it is connected to via its output connections.

Biological Plausibility

It is often overlooked that neural networks are highly abstracted versions of the neural networks found in real brains. Activation units only resemble real neurons in very general terms.

*Activation units emit a simple **numerical signal** whereas biological neurons emit a series of **pulses**.*

Similarly, brains are constructed from many different kinds of neuron, but neural networks tend to use just one type of activation unit.

Yet amazingly, even though artificial neural networks are gross simplifications of real neural networks, they share fundamental properties with their biological equivalents.

Parallel Distributed Processing

Computers are faster than brains. The basic components used by computer processors are much faster than biological neurons. The fastest neuron can transmit around 1000 signals per second. Electrical circuits can operate around a million times faster.

Despite this, brains carry out extremely complex operations amazingly fast – it only takes a tenth of a second to recognize your own mother!

Parallel vs. Serial Computation

The vast majority of digital computers compute *serially*. For example, to calculate the result of (1 + 4) + (4 x 8), a serial computer would first calculate (1 + 4) and get 5, next calculate (4 x 8) and get 32. It would then add these together to yield 37. The calculation is broken into a series of sub-calculations performed one after the other. An equivalent *parallel* computation would calculate (1 + 4) and (4 x 8) at the same time, thereby reducing the time required to perform the calculation. Constituent parts of the computation are calculated in *parallel*.

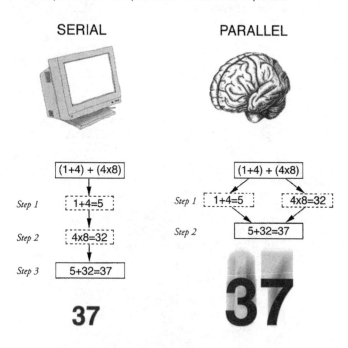

The brain is massively parallel, whereas most computers compute serially. This is why the brain is so fast, despite its relatively slow machinery. The property of parallelism present in neural networks makes connectionist models appealing. The manner in which they carry out the processing task is far closer to how the brain computes.

Robustness and Graceful Degradation

If you deliberately damage, even slightly, any part of your computer's main processing unit it will not work any more. Conventional computing machinery is not very robust. In contrast, slight brain damage will rarely result in someone dropping dead – it might even have no effect whatsoever. In fact, the ageing process itself results in neurons dying all the time.

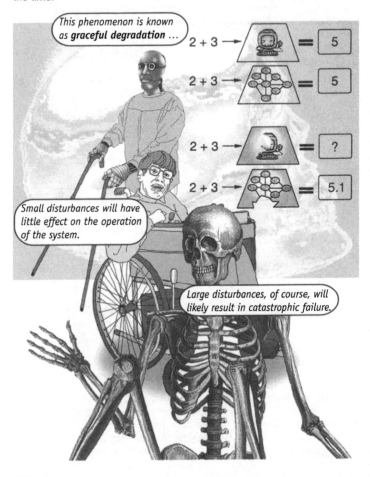

This phenomenon is known as **graceful degradation** ...

$2 + 3 \rightarrow$ = 5

$2 + 3 \rightarrow$ = 5

$2 + 3 \rightarrow$ = ?

$2 + 3 \rightarrow$ = 5.1

Small disturbances will have little effect on the operation of the system.

Large disturbances, of course, will likely result in catastrophic failure.

The important point is that the degree of degradation is in some sense proportional to the degree of damage to the system. Neural networks exhibit precisely this behaviour since each neuron acts as a separate processor.

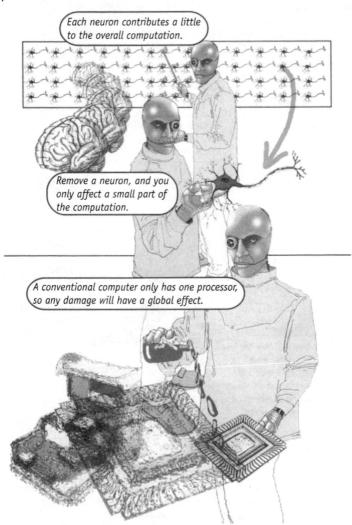

Each neuron contributes a little to the overall computation.

Remove a neuron, and you only affect a small part of the computation.

A conventional computer only has one processor, so any damage will have a global effect.

Machine Learning and Connectionism

Machine Learning is a branch of AI that spans both the classical symbolic approach and connectionism. Here, models of learning capture the ability of an agent to improve itself in light of information in the environment. Often, the ability of connectionist systems to learn is cited as one of its defining characteristics, and a feature most attractive to AI researchers.

But importantly, symbolic approaches are equally well suited to learning. The neural network approach to learning is best seen as adding to a long history of research into this core concern for AI.

Learning in Neural Networks

A wide variety of problems have been addressed using neural network learning mechanisms. On the basis of prior experience, neural networks can be trained to learn associations between patterns of experiences by altering the strength of the connections between activation units. For example, neural networks have been used to attack the following problems:

Making mortgage decisions

When you apply for a mortgage, the decision may well depend on the result of a neural network.

The mortgage company has trained the neural network on the basis of thousands of previous mortgage decisions.

The aim is to predict who will be a bad customer, and who will be a good one.

Categorizing sonar echoes

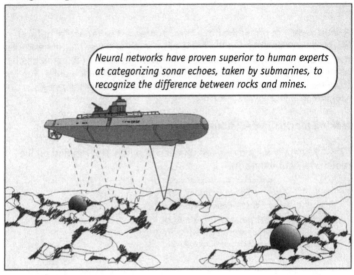

Learning to vocalize

One neural network, NETtalk, learns how to produce speech sounds from phonemes, the building blocks of words.

Playing checkers

Neural networks have been trained to play checkers, which, as we have seen, is a classic problem in AI traditionally solved using **symbolic** approaches.

Robot brains

Many robots rely on neural networks to control how their motor movements should react to sensor readings, for example, learning how to avoid obstacles.

Local Representations

Symbolic representations are the lynch-pin of classical AI. In a symbolic system, units of information are shunted around and operated on by the model.

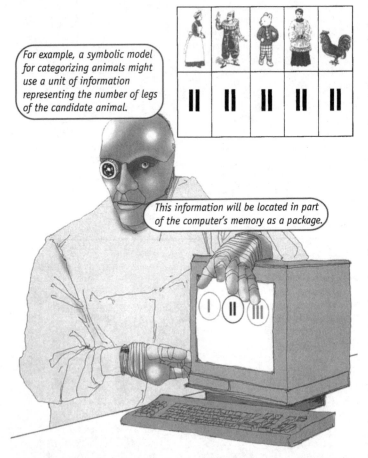

For example, a symbolic model for categorizing animals might use a unit of information representing the number of legs of the candidate animal.

This information will be located in part of the computer's memory as a package.

This kind of representation is termed a *local* representation because the information about the number of legs is kept together in a locatable package.

Distributed Representations

The kinds of information processing performed by neural networks can differ fundamentally in nature from those found in symbolic systems. Representations are often *distributed* in the same way that processing can be distributed. A distributed representation is spread out across the whole network, rather than being localized to a specific area or being built up from atomic units.

Information is not stored anywhere in particular. Rather it is stored everywhere.

Information is better thought of as "evoked" than "found".

Of course, neural networks themselves are built up from atomic units – artificial neurons – but these units are rarely used by the designer to represent anything in themselves.

Complex Activity

So, in a distributed representation, a single neuron is unlikely to be responsible for representing the number of legs of our candidate animal. Instead, the number of legs would be represented by a complex pattern of activity over a wide number of neurons. Some of these neurons will play a part in representing some other property in the system.

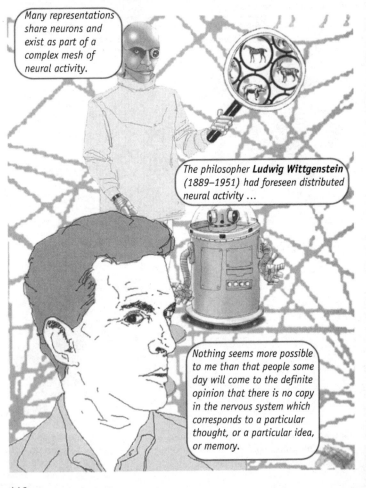

Many representations share neurons and exist as part of a complex mesh of neural activity.

The philosopher **Ludwig Wittgenstein** *(1889–1951) had foreseen distributed neural activity ...*

Nothing seems more possible to me than that people some day will come to the definite opinion that there is no copy in the nervous system which corresponds to a particular thought, or a particular idea, or memory.

Interpreting Distributed Representations

As a general rule, you can't locate specific items of information by pointing your finger at part of a distributed representation in the same way that you can with a local representation.

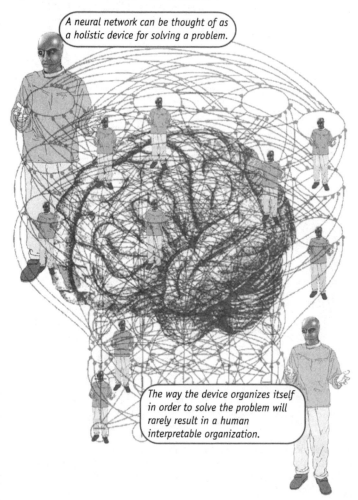

Complementary Approaches

Connectionism is often depicted as a revolution in AI – a flurry of new ideas concerning old problems, and a timely replacement for "Good old fashioned AI". Historically, both connectionism and symbolic AI have their roots in early work on AI. Independently of McCulloch and Pitts, Alan Turing had considered the idea of collections of artificial neurons acting as a computing device.

Alan Turing's insights on AI were profound, even more so if we consider his little-known pioneering work on connectionism.

*In the 1940s, I experimented with an idea of **unorganized machines** – quirky versions of what are now called neural networks.*

It was an accident of history that led to symbolic AI becoming the conceptual vocabulary of choice for so long. Despite recent bickering between the rival camps, most would now agree that the two approaches complement each other.

Can Neural Networks Think?

Searle's Chinese Room argument hinges on the idea that computers, as we know them today, can only manipulate meaningless symbols. The machine can never have an understanding of the symbols it manipulates. Agree or disagree with Searle, this issue is still a mystery. However, there are two reasons why connectionism could contribute to this debate.

First, neural networks differ substantially from conventional computers when physically instantiated ...

and my argument pivots on the inadequacy of classical physical machinery to support understanding.

Second, in a connectionist system, computation proceeds at a sub-symbolic level – the relationship between computation and symbolic atoms is less clear.

The Chinese Gym

Predictably, the resilient Searle stands firm and replies with the *Chinese Gym*. Instead of a room containing a lone Searle, he imagines a gym full of non-Chinese speakers, one for each neuron in the neural network.

However, the Chinese Gym does serve as an illustration that the whole can be more than the sum of the parts. In a sub-symbolic system, the atomic units, neurons and their structured relationship to other neurons, do not individually do much at all. Only when the collection is seen as a whole can we start to speak of concepts such as distributed representations and cognition.

Neural networks therefore exhibit the properties of emergence and self-organization discussed earlier.

The Symbol Grounding Problem

Searle's argument concerns the inability of the symbols being manipulated to mean anything. By themselves, symbols are meaningless shapes realized by, in the case of a conventional computer, a pattern of electrical activity. Any meaning we confer to the symbols is parasitic on the meaning in our heads.

What the psychologist Stevan Harnard terms the **symbol grounding problem** addresses this issue.

Meaning can enter the system only when part of the system is grounded in the world, rather than being part of a closed, self-referential system of symbols.

Harnard views connectionism as a good candidate for achieving this grounding, especially when coupled with a symbolic system.

Symbol Grounding

First, imagine a native English-speaker learning Chinese, armed only with a Chinese-Chinese dictionary. Harnard likens this to a cryptologist cracking a code.

You might break into the Chinese language, but this is contingent on an understanding of your own language.

The meaning of any Chinese you learn is parasitic on English.

Breaking the Circle

Could you ever learn Chinese as a first language, with only the aid of a Chinese-Chinese dictionary? Harnard likens this to a symbol–symbol merry-go-round.

Meaningless symbols are only ever defined in terms of other meaningless symbols.

This is exactly the position a machine is placed in.

How can symbols ever be grounded by anything but other meaningless symbols? Part of the problem of ascribing meaning to a symbol requires that the circle of meaninglessness be broken.

Harnard imagines a classical symbolic system sitting on top of a sub-symbolic connectionist system. Importantly, the connectionist system has inputs that are grounded in the outside world through sensors. In this way, symbolic representations are no longer defined in terms of other symbols, but are instead related to *iconic representations* which are directly linked to the sensory surfaces of the system.

> *A symbol representing **dog** takes its meaning from the complex of sensory images common to dogs ...*

> *Rather than other meaningless symbols such as **barks, has-four-legs** and **smells**.*

It is the connectionist system that supplies the sensory images. By combining symbolic and connectionist systems, Harnard believes we can begin to break out of the closed world of meaningless symbols that Searle discusses.

The Demise of AI?

The fact is, that after half a century of research into AI, the fruits of this research have failed to measure up to expectation. Arguably, we are not even approaching the goal of being able to build machines that can match the cognitive capacities of humans. The psychologist and philosopher Jerry Fodor has summed up the problem.

AI has walked into a game of 3-dimensional chess, thinking it was a tic-tac-toe.

Or as Rodney Brooks of MIT put it ...

Artificial Intelligence has foundered ... the symbol system hypothesis upon which classical AI is based is fundamentally flawed ...

This lack of progress has led practitioners of AI to take stock. Are the current approaches to AI misguided, or are we just around the corner from a breakthrough? A number of researchers suspect the former, and have actively sought to re-orientate AI.

"… the cognitivistic paradigm's neglect of the fact that intelligent agents live in a real physical world leads to significant shortcomings in explaining intelligence." – Rolf Pfeifer and Christian Scheier

AI's analysis of high-level cognitive processes in agents detached from the complexities of physical environments has been identified as the source of some of its deepest problems.

New AI

"We used to argue whether a machine could think. The answer is, 'No'. What thinks is a total circuit, including perhaps a computer, a man, and an environment. Similarly, we may ask whether a brain can think, and again the answer will be, 'No'. What thinks is a brain inside a man who is part of a system which includes an environment." – Gregory Bateson

This observation has led to the adoption of a new set of principles. This new orientation is not yet fully-fledged – it lacks a commonly used name, but is often termed *New AI*.

Far from being idle speculation, these new principles have resulted in impressive engineering projects.

But before examining new AI, it is important to analyse the array of problems conventional approaches to AI are accused of.

Micro-Worlds are Unlike the Everyday World

Measuring a theory against a simplified micro-world is a widespread practice in AI. Here, researchers distil what they believe to be the salient properties of a real environment into a virtual environment.

The success of an AI project is then measured relative to how humans would perform the same function in the everyday world.

Rarely are AI projects placed in the same situation as the human.

"Micro-worlds are not worlds but isolated meaningless domains, and it has gradually become clear that there is no way they could be combined and extended to arrive at the world of everyday life." – Hubert and Stuart Dreyfus

The Problems of Conventional AI

Scalability

Given that part of AI's goal is to establish *general* theories of intelligent action, this lack of scalability is a drawback that stands rank opposite to the goal of establishing general theories.

Robustness

A trait common to many AI systems, and that which is addressed by the CYC project, is the inability of many systems to react well to unforeseen circumstances. AI systems will often fail in the face of a novel situation. It is very hard to design a system robust enough to meet all eventualities. Humans and animals, on the other hand, rarely suffer from this problem.

Operating in Real-Time

The sense-model-plan-act cycle that underlies the design of conventional intelligent agents leads to massive amounts of information-processing. Before a change in the environment can be reacted to, sensory information must pass through the complex processes of modelling, planning, and then acting. This complex loop of information-flow makes keeping up with the world extremely hard. Shakey is a good example of this phenomenon.

My behaviour was characterized by long pauses during which complex information-processing was carried out.

Humans and animals, in contrast, react very quickly to events going on around them.

This would indicate that something other than "sense-model-plan-act" is going on.

In one sense, the problem of creating intelligent agents has already been solved. Over the course of the earth's 4.5 billion years of history, evolution has solved the problem over and over again. Mammals arrived 370 million years ago. Our last common ancestor with the apes started milling around 5 million years ago.

How did evolution do it?

Biological evolution builds on existing designs by adding the occasional improvement.

Starting with the basics – beasts capable of surviving in an environment and then reproducing – evolution has built layer upon layer of extra machinery over millions of years.

The New Argument from Evolution

The MIT roboticist Rodney Brooks takes the evolutionary basics as evidence that "hard" tasks like reasoning, planning and language might turn out to be easier to understand once the basics are in place.

Intelligence is contingent on the ability to react to an environment.

Can our knowledge of evolution inform AI? Brooks believes that it can, and argues that we should first aim to build basic mechanical creatures before we try to build mechanical humans.

The Argument from Biology

The intimate relationship between an organism and its environment has been noted and studied by biologists since the 19th century. Yet AI is rarely informed by the insights of biologists. For example, in the work of Humberto R. Maturana and Francisco J. Varela, the neural circuitry found in the retina of the eye of a frog is shown to excite in the presence of blob-like structures that resemble flies.

In studying its behaviour, we might want to attribute to the frog an "internal model of the world" that contains flies, and, say, other frogs.

But this simply is not the kind of phenomenon that exists in the everyday world of a frog.

Non-Cognitive Behaviour

Maturana and Varela illustrate this point by first presenting a juicy fly to the top-left area of the frog's field of view.

Next, they sever part of the frog's eye, such that the whole eye can be rotated by 180 degrees.

Importantly, the frog will persist with this behaviour. It will never adapt its behaviour in light of the unsuccessful attempts to capture the fly.

The moral of the story is that a frog's eye does not act as a camera supplying information to the frog's planning module, which then constructs a plan to catch the fly.

Instead, as Maturana and Varela went on to show, the fly-catching behaviour is solved by the *retina itself*, independent of the processes going on in the rest of the frog's brain. This experiment illustrates how certain behaviours, such as foraging for food, are realized through a tight coupling between perception and action, independent of, and without the need for, any high-level cognitive processes.

The Argument from Philosophy

Many of the concepts central to AI have their roots in the work of philosophers such as Descartes, Hobbes, Leibniz, as we have seen, and the *Tractatus Logico-Philosophicus* of **Ludwig Wittgenstein** (1889–1951):

The world is the totality of facts, not of things.

We argued that it was possible to arrive at a formal theory of the everyday world, based on a collection of **formal primitives.**

AI translated this idea into the language of symbolic information processing ...

Equip a computer with an appropriate set of primitives, and it should be able to function in the world, in the same way that a human does.

Against Formalism

Wittgenstein, in his later philosophy, and **Martin Heidegger** (1889–1976) strongly reject the formalist assumption of meaning.

But what are the simple constituent parts of which reality is composed? ... It makes no sense at all to speak absolutely of the "simple parts of a chair".

We took issue with the assumption that it is possible to talk of "meaningful" mental representations, detached from the activity of experience.

A formal theory, they claimed, is by its very nature detached from the activity that gives it any meaning.

This alternative philosophical standpoint suggests that our interpretation of the world cannot be made explicit, and any attempt to do so will render our insights grossly inaccurate.

No Disembodied Intelligence

This argument formed the backbone of one of the foremost critiques of AI. The philosopher Hubert Dreyfus, in the 1970s, declared that AI was misguided in its assumption that disembodied intelligence was possible. On the perceived failure of classical AI, Dreyfus noted ...

The rationalist tradition had finally been put to an empirical test, and it had failed. The idea of producing a formal, atomistic theory of the everyday commonsense world and of representing that theory in a symbol manipulator had run into just the difficulties Heidegger and Wittgenstein had discovered.

Agents in the Real World

Can AI learn anything useful from this philosophical debate? If Heidegger, Wittgenstein and Dreyfus are correct in their rejection of disembodied intelligence, then AI must begin to focus on how the behaviour of an agent is constrained and partially determined by the activities it engages in.

This focus suggests that agents should be modelled not as disembodied, detached and isolated, but rather as engaged in the everyday world.

Dreyfus' critique was initially scoffed at by the AI community, but is increasingly becoming an acceptable topic for debate.

The New AI

The arguments from evolution, biology and philosophy stand in opposition to much of conventional AI research. But to put these arguments into practice, they need to be translated into engineering principles. Three principles characterize the new approach to AI.

The First Principle of Embodiment

Embodiment is the idea that having a body is **theoretically** significant.

That is, the constraints a body places on an agent are crucial to how it interacts in the world.

The degree to which embodiment is significant remains a controversial issue. Rodney Brooks goes as far as to say, "Intelligence requires a body." For example, the design of a robot body will determine the sensory phenomena it experiences.

The Second Principle of Situatedness

Situatedness refers to an agent being located in a complex environment, rather than a highly abstracted micro-world. The complexities of real environments are taken to be fundamentally different from those of the abstracted "micro-worlds". Indeed, being situated permits the exploiting of structure in the world, lessening the burden of internal representations.

Elsie, Walter's robotic tortoise, exploited the location of the recharging station inside the hutch.

No model of the hutch is ever invoked by Elsie. Its function was the result of the interaction between Elsie's sensors and the real-world.

Rodney Brooks sums up this kind of relationship by arguing that "the world is its own best model".

The Third Principle of Bottom-Up Design

Given the goal of building an intelligent agent, the methodology frequently adopted by AI is to build from the top downwards.

That is, higher-level functions such as knowledge and reasoning are targeted first, with lower-level functions swept under the carpet until later.

*New AI proposes **bottom-up** design. Start with the basics first ...*

For example, Rodney Brooks builds basic machines analogous to insects. His idea is that only by understanding the basics first can we begin to understand the complexities of human cognition.

Behaviour-Based Robotics

The principles of new AI are put into exemplary practice by Rodney Brooks. Brooks has spearheaded an approach known as behaviour-based robotics.

I wish to build completely autonomous mobile agents that co-exist in the world with humans, and are seen by those humans as intelligent beings in their own right. I will call such agents Creatures ...

Using bottom-up design, how would Brooks succeed in building simple robotic creatures that resemble insects?

Behaviours as Units of Design

*Evolution builds layer upon layer. It is incremental. It fine tunes and elaborates on **existing designs** to yield new designs.*

*Behaviour-based robotics is inspired by such an approach. Its units of design are **behaviours**.*

Behaviours are built on, to yield more complex behaviours. Unlike much of conventional robotics, which takes the sense-model-plan-act cycle as a starting point, Brooks' robots contain pieces of machinery that are autonomous and operate in parallel. *There is no central control.* These behaviours implement a tight coupling between perception and action, and avoid the use of cognitive processes to mediate between perception and action.

The Robot Genghis

In the 1980s, Brooks and his colleagues built Genghis, a six-legged robot. Genghis was designed to walk across challenging environments and seek out the infrared glow emitted by humans and other animals. Genghis was a success for two reasons.

First, I could negotiate challenging terrain, just as an insect can.

After studying video-footage of insect movements, I built a machine that moved successfully, much like an insect.

Second, Brooks achieved this by using novel techniques.

Genghis has no central control. Nowhere in his construction is there a description of *how to walk*. "The software for Genghis was not organized as a single program but rather as fifty-one little tiny parallel programs."

Behaviour by Design

Genghis is composed of many simple autonomous behaviours, organized as layers of control. Each layer introduces more refined and controlled behaviour.

For example, one layer encapsulates the behaviour of **standing up.**

Another layer then captures the rudiments of walking, such as **leg swinging** and **leg coordination.**

Additional layers help to make Genghis increasingly robust.

The construction design of Genghis is a function of the kind of terrain in which he has to operate. The behaviours given to Genghis were strongly influenced by the constraints imposed by his body.

Collections of Agents

Although the principles of new AI translate most directly into the field of robotics, they are by no means limited to issues in robotics. A closer treatment of the interaction between agents and their environments can be applied to every branch of AI. Luc Steels, director of the AI Lab at the University of Brussels, takes another line to the "bottom-up" approach by investigating the evolution of both meaning and communication systems in *collections of agents*.

In this approach, the human designer does not put his or her language and concepts into the agents, but tries to set up systems that autonomously generate their own.

The Talking Heads Experiment

The agents in the Talking Heads experiment exist independently of any physical robot. They are located in a virtual environment supported by a computer network spanning many physical locations. When agents need to interact with each other, they become grounded in the everyday world by teleporting to robotic bodies at physical locations such as Brussels, Paris or London.

By borrowing robotic bodies when needed, the Talking Heads experiment can support many agents, even though the number of robotic bodies may be limited.

These robotic bodies are called **Talking Heads**.

THE WORLD

They are composed of a camera, a loudspeaker and a microphone. Talking Heads act as a robotic shell that the virtual agents can occupy when they need to.

Categorizing Objects

The aim of the experiment is to investigate how a shared language can emerge as a result of the interactions between agents. Crucially, nowhere in the experiment is language defined; it develops as a result of interactions between the agents. Starting with a blank slate, the agents autonomously develop their own "ontologies" – a sense of being in the world – that allow them to identify and discriminate between objects in the real world.

As soon as agents develop the ability to categorize objects, they attempt to name the objects by communicating with each other.

The agents' categorization of the world is not programmed but emerges. It is constructed and learned by the agents themselves.

The Naming Game

Steels' agents interact by playing language games. A language game can start when two different agents are selected and then teleported to the same physical location. Sitting in two separate robotic bodies, both agents view the same scene from different positions. Each scene comprises a number of coloured shapes on a white-board.

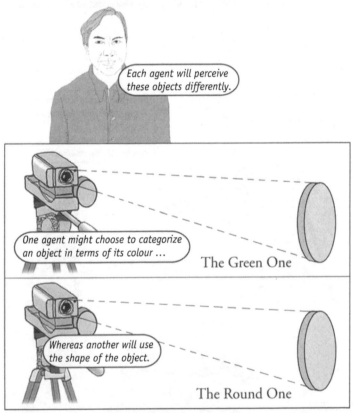

Agents arrive at different conceptions of the world due to the fact that they always occupy slightly different locations, and focus on different objects over the course of their lifetime. For this reason, agents develop their own ontologies.

Once agents can categorize objects in the scenes they are exposed to, they begin to play language games. The two agents first agree on a context, which is some part of the scene they are viewing. One of the agents speaks to another, by forming an utterance that identifies one of the objects in the context.

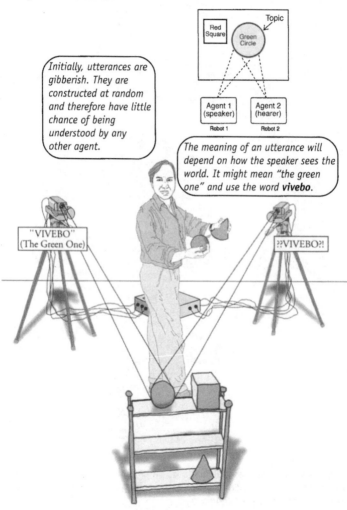

Initially, utterances are gibberish. They are constructed at random and therefore have little chance of being understood by any other agent.

The meaning of an utterance will depend on how the speaker sees the world. It might mean "the green one" and use the word **vivebo**.

"VIVEBO" (The Green One)

??VIVEBO?!

A Feedback Process

The hearer then tries to understand what is meant by the other's *vivebo* and points to what it thinks is being identified.

In this way, the set of signals used by an agent to refer to objects in the world is either reinforced or revised, depending on the feedback gained from playing language games.

Self-Organization in Cognitive Robots

The key insight of the Talking Heads experiment is that agents develop their own individual and internal way of categorising the world they see. While, at the same time, through external communication, they negotiate a *shared lexicon*. Different agents may be talking about the same object, but they might conceptualize it differently, yet at the same time share words. Steels' experiment illustrates how a communication system, grounded in the everyday world, can emerge through interactions between agents, yet not be defined in any one of them.

The Future

Practitioners of AI often make bold predictions.

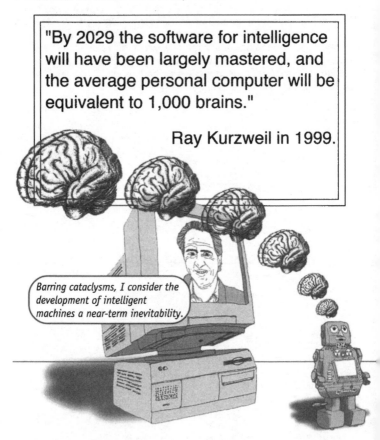

"By 2029 the software for intelligence will have been largely mastered, and the average personal computer will be equivalent to 1,000 brains."

Ray Kurzweil in 1999.

Barring cataclysms, I consider the development of intelligent machines a near-term inevitability.

These claims, considered in light of the fact that there is little evidence so far to suggest that anything approaching human intelligence is possible in machines, are premature. Scientists have a habit of predicting that breakthroughs will occur around the time of their retirement. It is hard, therefore, to take seriously claims of AI reaching its goal in the near future.

"In stark contrast to the largely unanticipated explosion of computers into the mainstream, the entire endeavour of robotics has failed rather completely to live up to the predictions of the 1950s."

Hans Moravec

Most people know what robots are and could perhaps even name a famous one.

But other than industrial robots which are widespread in, for example, the car construction industry, robots are rarely seen outside research laboratories. Useful robots have failed to materialize.

The Nearer Future

However, there is evidence that robots will start to become more widespread, moving out of the research laboratories and into the everyday world.

In discussing the future prospects of AI, it is wise therefore to look at what is likely in the near future and compare these insights with what researchers are claiming is possible further down the line.

The Sony Dream Robot

In early 2002, the SONY Corporation announced the development of the Sony Dream Robot (SDR), a prototype humanoid robot. The capabilities of the SDR far outstrip any other bipedal robot.

A walking robot could feasibly live in a house and carry out chores in places that the more common wheeled robots cannot reach.

All Singing, All Dancing

What makes the SDR impressive is its robustness. Walking robots have been developed before but were often restricted by only being able to accomplish limited patterns of behaviour, and they were mostly subject to remote control by a human.

If the SDR falls over, it gets itself up, just as a human would.

The SDR also avoids obstacles using a stereo vision system, rather than stupidly bumping into obstacles as it goes.

The SDR is aimed at the entertainment market. Apart from walking around, the SDR can sing, dance, and recognize faces and voices.

Sony's objective is for the SDR to interact with its owners by striking up an emotional bond.

"In addition to short-term memory functions to temporarily memorize individuals and objects, SDR-4X is equipped with long-term memory functions to memorize faces and names through more in-depth communications with people. Emotional information based on a communication experience will be memorized on a long-term memory as well. By utilizing both short and long-term memories, the SDR-4X achieves more complicated conversations and performances." – SONY Corporation Press Release

The SDR is a Serious Robot

While SONY's Dream Robot is very impressive, can it really shed light on AI's objective of understanding cognition by building machines? One important outcome of projects like the SDR is that they provide a platform on which other AI technologies can be explored. Taking Brooks' maxim of "intelligence requires a body", the availability of an off-the-shelf body may prove very useful.

For example, Luc Steels, in conjunction with the SONY Corporation, has a project planned to combine the Talking Heads Experiment with the SONY SDR-4X.

The aim here is to allow the owner and the SDR to develop a communication system of their own.

By verbally interacting with the robot, human and robot will meet in the middle ...

... by developing a basic communication system.

Future Possibilities

Based on the projected likelihood of widely available machinery of sufficient power, the well-known roboticist Hans Moravec has predicted in detail the next four generations of robots. It is important to stress that some practitioners of AI see these predictions as nothing more than science fiction, with little evidence so far to suggest they are remotely likely.

The path I've outlined roughly recapitulates the evolution of human intelligence – but 100 million times more rapidly.

It suggests that robot intelligence will surpass our own well before 2050.

Moravec imagines four generations of *Universal Robots*, so named because they will be universally available, in the same way that desktop computers are today. Once robots become useful and affordable, Moravec predicts they will be far more widespread than computers. There are more uses for robots than computers.

Moravec's Prediction

1st Generation

By 2010, robots built from machinery capable of 3,000 MIPS (million instructions per second) will be used universally. These robots will have lizard-scale intellect coupled with a humanoid body.

2nd Generation

By 2020, computing power will increase to 100,000 MIPS, capturing mouse-scale intellect.

3rd Generation

By 2030, computing power will reach 3,000,000 MIPS. This kind of machinery can realize what Moravec terms monkey-scale intellect.

4th Generation

By 2040, with machinery capable of 100,000,000 MIPS, human-scale intellect will be upon us.

Fact or Fiction? Moravec's predictions are extremely bold and many would disagree with him. Progress towards AI has repeatedly fallen short of the progress made in building more advanced computing machinery. For this reason, Moravec's claims should be taken as the absolute best case scenario.

AI: A New Kind of Evolution?

Assuming that Strong AI is possible, and we believe the predictions of some well-known scientists, a new kind of evolution will occur. Instead of producing biological offspring, we will instead begin to produce what Hans Moravec calls *mind-children* – engineered beings superior to us.

Information is transmitted from generation to generation by two forms of evolution.

Biological *evolution results in the transmission of information required for building a human. This information is encoded in our genes.*

Cultural *evolution results in the transmission of concepts and practices such as science, religion, art and so on. This information is transmitted from mind to mind by storage codes and learning from others.*

Both biological and cultural evolution result in information persisting from generation to generation.

By engineering our own offspring, many have proposed that Artificial Intelligence can lead to the *Lamarckian evolution* of our species. In contrast to Darwin's theory of evolution by natural selection, Lamarck proposed that evolution allows characteristics acquired over our lifetime to be transmitted to future generations.

Evolution Without Biology

By engineering our own offspring we can alter their design. The acquired ability to reproduce ourselves will affect our evolution. In this way, the rate of evolution could increase.

"An evolutionary process accelerates because it builds on its own means for further evolution. Humans have beaten evolution. We are creating intelligent entities in considerably less time than it took the evolutionary process that created us." – Ray Kurzweil

Our evolution will for the first time be separated from, and be totally independent of, biological constraints.

Culture will then evolve independently of biology – and far more quickly.

"In the past we have tended to see ourselves as a final product of evolution, but our evolution has not ceased. Indeed, we are now evolving more rapidly ... based on inventive kinds of 'unnatural selection'." – Marvin Minsky

If AI's goal of exposing humans as mere machines succeeds, then we will no longer suffer the restrictions of our organic machinery. Humans, and intelligent machinery in the widest sense, could then, in theory, evolve outside the restrictions of biological evolution.

A Forecast

Many would argue that Moravec's view of the future of AI is unlikely. The arrival dates of his universal robots are particularly bold. At the beginning of this book, it was noted that AI's history can be viewed in terms of the progress of two strands of research: research into *robotics* and research into the general question of *cognitive capacities*.

Robots are about to become widely available.

Large companies, such Sony and Honda, are investing heavily in useful robots.

At the time of writing, an affordable robot vacuum cleaner has just come onto the market. Robotics is stepping out of the academic research lab and into the world of global industry. This move promises real progress. It is unlikely that an engineering project as advanced as the Sony Dream Robot could have been developed in an academic setting.

Mechanized Cognition

Endowing machines with cognitive capacities is quite another matter and remains a huge problem. The majority of AI practitioners are likely to continue to explore AI by taking the classical and connectionist routes.

These older AI approaches are now well established.

But new AI, based on the observation that intelligent activity is the result of a complex interaction between agent and environment, should continue to gain acceptance.

Without the insights of new AI, it is hard to see where breakthroughs will come from.

The Future Meeting of the Paths

If the principles that define new AI prove to be insightful, then AI will need to situate agents in far richer environments that reflect the phenomena dealt with by humans and animals. AI investigates cognition in agents. At the same time, it has largely failed to appreciate that evolution has already solved that problem.

Traditionally, AI has failed to recognize the importance of the interactions between agent and environment.

Many practitioners of AI are beginning to believe that these interactions are fundamental. Taking this idea to its limit will require AI to work with either robotic bodies or more informed micro-worlds. So far, AI has treated environmental complexity as a secondary issue. Micro-worlds are designed using nothing more than guesswork.

Further Reading

For a good general introduction to Artificial Intelligence, the following books are respected and well written. Pfeifer and Scheier offer an up-to-date and thorough treatment of the big issues in AI.

- Rolf Pfeifer and Christian Scheier, *Understanding Intelligence* (Cambridge, MA: MIT Press, 2001).
- Roger Penrose, *The Emperor's New Mind: Concerning Computers, Minds, and the Laws of Physics* (Oxford: Oxford University Press, 1989).

These two collections of articles offer an accessible route to some of the key philosophical issues.

- Douglas R. Hofstadter and Daniel C. Dennett, *The Mind's I: Fantasies and Reflections on Self and Soul* (New York, NY: Basic Books, 1981).
- John Haugeland (ed.), *Mind Design II: Philosophy, Psychology, and Artificial Intelligence* (Cambridge, MA: MIT Press, 1997).

The next two books are excellent introductions to Artificial Intelligence for those interested in AI from the perspective of computer programming. They cover the technical foundations of AI.

- Stuart Russell and Peter Norvig, *Artificial Intelligence: A Modern Approach* (Harlow: Prentice Hall, 1994).
- Nils J. Nilsson, *Artificial Intelligence: A New Synthesis* (San Francisco, CA: Morgan Kaufmann, 1998).

The following two books are written by leading roboticists, and target the general reader. For those interested in robotics, these books offer a good place to start from.

- Rodney Brooks, *Robot: The Future of Flesh and Machines* (London: Penguin, 2002).
- Hans Moravec, *Robot: Mere Machine to Transcendent Mind* (Oxford: Oxford University Press, 1999).

Index

The Author and Artist

Henry Brighton has carried out research into machine learning in both academic and commercial settings. More recently, his work has focused on the problem of the evolution of language, where he employs machine learning techniques to model linguistic evolution in multi-agent populations.

Howard Selina was born in Leeds and studied painting at St. Martin's School of Art and the Royal Academy. He works in London as a painter and illustrator, and having sorted out the old steel boat he is currently renovating an old stone house in West Yorkshire. This is his fourth book for Icon.

Acknowledgements

The author would like to thank Luc Steels of the AI Lab at Vrije Universiteit Brussel. The members of the Language Evolution and Computation Research Unit at the University of Edinburgh also helped greatly, in particular, Joseph Poulshock, Kenny Smith and Andrew Smith. The author is also grateful for the understanding of Simon Kirby and Jim Hurford, and for the advice offered by Anna Claybourne, Jelle Zuidema and Paul Vogt.

The artist would like to thank Richard Appignanesi for his ideas and suggestions, and for not panicking, and Ms Paola di Giancroce for her cups of tea, glasses of wine, and bicycle outings.